LEGACY THOUGHTS TO LIVE BY
By Jim Fite

"YOU make a difference in others' lives"

INTRODUCTION

After our company, the Judge Fite Companies, had been in business for 85 years and I celebrated my fiftieth year in the real estate business, Dermot Buffini and the founder of RIS Media, John Featherston, interviewed me for their RIS Media live webinar event, *"Lessons on Leadership."* They asked me to share some of my knowledge that others could use to build their real estate and related companies and enrich people's lives in a positive way throughout the world.

During the event, I shared with the audience what my father taught me when I wanted to quit my college education and join the real estate brokerage world at the young age of eighteen years old. He, Judge B. Fite, and my mother, Dene Fite, gave me two requirements for quitting college and getting my real estate license.

Dad said, "Son, you NEVER stop learning!" And he followed that statement up with these two requirements:

1. Read, study, and think for an hour a day, five days a week for the rest of your life.
2. Go to school, sit in a classroom, at least one day per month, or an average of twelve days per year for the rest of your life.

What I didn't realize was Dermot picked up on these requirements during the webinar and later called to challenge me to put pen to paper and write my legacy.

What would I want to tell the world, my country, my community, my family, my friends, my company-- and most importantly--my grandchildren?

And so, the next morning, I began writing my legacy "thoughts." Each one is an important focus for me at this point in my life. In this book, I have summed up a few of the various lessons I learned from continuing to build my spiritual journey, family, company, and friendships along the way.

My Personal Mission: To be a positive example to others by spiritually living life, family values, giving to others, career success, and financial stability.

THANK YOU, DERMOT, for inspiring me and making a difference in all the people you touch and the lives you help change.

Table of Contents

CHAPTER 1   1
YOU make a difference in others' lives!

CHAPTER 2   8
GOD is around YOU at all times... YOU are NEVER alone!

CHAPTER 3   11
YOUR family is your legacy... they are always watching and learning!

CHAPTER 4   15
LOVE is the most positive emotion on earth... and LOVE is within YOU!

CHAPTER 5   18
YOU are made to work... to contribute to others and to the world!

CHAPTER 6   26
Be FREE from debt... FREE your body, mind, and soul!

CHAPTER 7   31
BEGIN... the rest is easy!

CHAPTER 8   34
Worry... is wasted mind power!

CHAPTER 9   38
Ask questions... LISTEN to the answers!

CHAPTER 10   41
Over communicating is KEY... Don't under-communicate and regret it!

CHAPTER 11   **45**
YOU have a choice every day... be HAPPY, have a GREAT DAY!

CHAPTER 12   **48**
ONE hour a day... read, study, and think!

CHAPTER 13   **52**
Classroom and world knowledge... ALWAYS keep learning!

CHAPTER 14   **56**
Money comes and money goes... it is the PEOPLE you touch and your REPUTATION you leave behind

CHAPTER 15   **61**
STRATEGIC planning and DAILY Affirmations

CHAPTER 1
YOU make a difference in others' lives!

This legacy statement will be my gift to the world. I don't remember if I came up with this quote or heard it from someone else and adopted it for myself. I tried researching it but was unable to find its originator. Therefore, I will claim it.

The interesting thing about this quote is that it can be framed as positive or negative!

POSITIVE –
I choose to think of the world, the United States of America, the great State of Texas, the Dallas/Fort Worth Metroplex, my family, my friends, and all those I meet as an opportunity to make a positive difference in the lives of others.

Each of us--YOU in particular--make a difference in others. How? By your thoughts, words, and actions. The Bible says, *"It is more blessed to give than to receive."* (Acts 20:35) YOU and I make a difference by giving a little piece of ourselves, our lives, to others.

How do YOU give? Random acts of kindness? Speaking an uplifting thought? A kind word? Helping someone less fortunate? Sharing a meal? Telling hard things because the receiver needs to hear it? Offering money to those who have had a catastrophic event in their life?

RANDOM ACTS OF KINDNESS – One Saturday morning, my wife Petey and I went to a privately owned coffee shop that we frequently visit for their light breakfast.

This particular morning the owner was visibly distracted and distressed about something. She was usually extremely pleasant and talkative to the patrons in the coffee shop. However, that morning she was absorbed in something that was troubling her.

Petey and I decided to care for her with our thoughts. Then as we left the coffee shop, we chose to go one step further. We went across the street to get her some flowers. As we gave her the bouquet, we realized the smile on her face was worth all the money in the world. It was at that moment we chose to look for opportunities to bless, opportunities to give, continually performing RANDOM ACTS OF KINDNESS!

OPPORTUNITIES surround YOU all the time--on a regular basis--wherever YOU are! Open your eyes to them, watch for them, and then act on the opportunities before you. A bouquet of flowers, a smile, a gift, a positive word, a helping hand. Blessing another person will in turn bring a blessing of happiness and fulfillment upon YOU.

Question – Will YOU start looking for the opportunities that surround you to give RANDOM ACTS OF KINDNESS?

INTENTIONAL ACTS OF KINDNESS – We all know people who are ill, physically or mentally. Recently one of my best friends on this earth was diagnosed with leukemia. He and I have been friends for 49 years. We have stood beside each other through marriage, divorce, him losing his wife in a 4-wheeler accident and raising our great group of kids.

For over forty years, we have been in business together and built our wealth by learning from each other. Through it all, the ups and downs of life, we remained best friends!

One day he called me. "Jim, I just heard from my doctor. He asked where I was and said, 'Drop everything and go directly to the hospital. You have leukemia and we will be starting treatment immediately.' Jim, I am on my way to the hospital."

He was there for fifty-two days in three different hospital rooms. Every doctor, nurse, cook in the kitchen, and people who cleaned his room "made a difference" in his life! His fiancé was there morning, noon, and night by his side, helping him, serving him, and giving him the physical and emotional support he needed.

True to who he was, while he was fighting for his life, he was ministering to the doctors, nurses, and anyone taking care of him! He was making a difference in others' lives! He continues to inspire me!

At this writing, pretty much every day—even this morning as I am working on this chapter—I send him a text, "How are you today?" He responds with the happenings of the day. It was my privilege to spend four days and nights in the hospital room with him. Whether he needed ice, water, food, or anything else, he received it. I was reminded of the time I spent with my father in the hospital when he had 1/3 of his lung removed during his bout with lung cancer. I guess my father's experience was the training ground for this experience. My father, through his illness and recovery, made a difference in my life, so I could make a difference in someone else's life.

When asked, *"How are you doing my friend?"* He says, *"Leukemia is a marathon, not a sprint."* At this point in my writing, he was running the marathon with the help, support, and prayers of his family, friends, and the entire company. He was in God's hands and the hands of modern medicine.

On May 9, 2022, seven months after the diagnosis, God took my friend home to be in Heaven with his loved ones who preceded him. I miss him terribly. He made a difference in others' lives until he passed away at M.D Anderson Hospital--he made a difference in my life!

Call someone you LOVE today--NOW--and tell them, *"I LOVE YOU!"*

It is a privilege to be able to serve, to give, and to LOVE!

STRONG LOVE - There is a time when you might have to give "tough LOVE." One of my family members had a physical and mental issue. The entire family rallied around to come up with the best possible care and solution for this family member and our family as a whole. Time and money were invested in the rehabilitation and prayers were lifted up for years. It took months through rehab and years of "tough LOVE" to get through this trial of life. Yet, it was all worth it! Our LOVE, making the "right" decisions on the family member's part coupled with God's grace conquered all!

Recently, Texas had a 100-year ice and snowstorm where much of the state lost its power for several days when temperatures fell below freezing. We soon found out how interdependent we as people are on each other. Food was hoarded, firewood was scarce, communication was out, and it was COLD. In Dallas/Fort Worth, it was down to "0" degrees! Yet, what happened was remarkable. Those who had power welcomed their neighbors over for a visit--sometimes turning into several days of cohabitating! Neighbors delivered firewood to those who needed it while others shared their food and water. Each person made a difference in someone else's life!

NEGATIVE –
You can also make a disruptive difference by being a negative influence on others like talking behind someone's back. Crushing someone's dreams with negative verbal communications. Telling someone that they "can't do something/anything right." Giving negative vibes . . .

How many dreams have been smothered by someone who is jealous of someone else? There is no doubt that jealousy is one of the seven deadly sins. Why is it that people don't want others to succeed? Why is it that people are jealous of what others have, their looks, jobs, friends, kids, co-workers, or financial stability? What good comes from this jealousy?

The actions that you and I do can directly help or hurt others. It is our choice in what we say, how we say it, when we say it, where we say it, whom we say it to, and most importantly, why we say it.

It has been said, *"No man (or woman) is an island."* We are all intertwined with each other. We all need each other and depend on each other.

And then there is gossip! Talking about someone behind their back. Talking untruths about someone. Gossip has killed relationships, marriages, families, companies, and yes, even countries. How many people have been hurt by someone's false rumor--gossip?

Zig Ziglar used to say, *"Be a GOOD FINDER!"* Find the good in people. We all have good in us; just look deeper if you cannot find it at first glance.

My mother, Dene Fite, said, *"If you can't say something nice, don't say anything at all."* Your mother probably said the same thing to you.

So, as you go through life, find the good, speak the good, and keep the negative out of your mind and mouth!

The question really is . . .

Will <u>YOU</u> make a difference by helping and serving others?

OR

Will you make a difference in hurting others?

It is your choice, all day, every day, today!

YOU make a difference in others' lives!

CHAPTER 2
GOD is around YOU at all times . . . YOU are NEVER alone!

Has anyone had a teenager or known a teenager very well? If so, you have watched this person you LOVE go through life's changes and challenges during their formative years, attempting to find themselves and their place in the world. The peer pressure, their parent's lack of brains, the condemnation of family members, and the ability to "think" they know everything about pretty much every single thing!

And yet, this young person is very much alone in their thinking. They are scared. In many cases, they isolate themselves from others. They stay cooped up in their room or go off by themselves. Their thoughts are wide and varied. What is life all about? Why am I on this earth? Why do people act the way they act?

They wonder, "Why?" "Why me?" "Why not me?" "Who LOVES me?" "Nobody LOVES me." "Why don't people LOVE me?" "Where do I belong?" "How do I get out of this . . . (funk)?" "Where can I go to not feel this way?"

I believe that no teenager, nor you or I, are alone--ever! There is a God that is all-knowing and all-LOVING! He is with us always and forever. Whenever we do good and whenever we don't do so well. Whatever our free will does, God is with us--always!

Bottom line--He forgives us of all our wrongdoings when we ask for forgiveness. God wants the very best for us. He is a LOVING God.

This teenager, and all of us, should rest our heads and hearts in the peace that our God gives us. When we talk with the Lord and pray to Him, He will listen to our wishes. He may, or may not, answer prayer in the way that we ask or in the timeframe we want. Yet He is always there and listening.

Looking back on my life, the challenges, and the opportunities that I prayed for, my God knew what was best for me and all those around me. He has a master plan for every teenager, young adult, mother, father, empty nester, for you and for me!

My God is always with me! Your God is and will always be with you . . . no matter what the circumstances.

I realize that this chapter may not fit within everyone's beliefs. Either YOU believe there is a supreme being or you do not. Maybe this will be the positive influence that will lead you to a life with Christ. I believe there is a God. I believe my God, who is very personal to me, is my creator and redeemer. I believe He gives me the power and free will to choose my path on this earth. I believe He gives me a mind to think with and a body in which to take action. He gives me a choice called FREE-WILL. I also believe that He sent the only perfect human being, Jesus Christ, to earth as man to give me an example of living an abundant and perfect life. He even died for my sins--and I have had my share for sure.

God is always with YOU!

YOU make a difference in others' lives!

CHAPTER 3
YOUR family is your legacy . . . they are always watching and learning!

I was fortunate to grow up in a home with a mother and father who LOVED one another and their four children. After living on this earth for many years, owning a business filled with people from around the globe, and traveling much of the world, I realized that not everyone grew up in a home like I did. Yes, I was blessed.

Throughout my life I have asked questions, listened, shared, coached, suggested professional help, and been the recipient of advice from those who are wiser and smarter.

They say experience is the best teacher. I say, learn from other people who have already had the experiences of life. Listen to their wisdom. There are so many people whom you can count on to give you good advice. Go to them, ask them, and most importantly, LISTEN. Then take the "right" action to accomplish great things in life!

I do believe in the opportunity we all have to change the legacy of our family forever! This pertains to both a positive and negative reflection.

We all come from "dysfunctional families" in our own way. Yes, even my "perfect" family is dysfunctional. Why? Because none of our families or family members are perfect! We all have flaws. We all have strengths and weaknesses. We are all HUMAN and we all falter.

So, the question is, "How do we create a positive legacy for our family members?"

No, I am not a psychiatrist or psychologist. I am merely a person who has lived life, watched, and communicated with thousands of employees, friends, and family members. I learned and applied great lessons from them!

YOUR family is YOUR legacy:

- What will you do to improve the direction of your family tree?
- What will you do to teach your children and grandchildren?
- What will you do to live your life more abundantly for them to follow?
- How do you give them spiritual guidance?
- How do you act when they are looking?
- How do you act when you think they are not looking?
- It is your choice, not your spouse, your kids, your parents, or friends--it is YOUR CHOICE!

YOUR family is watching. How are you influencing your family through your actions?

When my first grandson was born, I started sending him emails (through his parents) that turned into LOVE LETTERS. They were thoughts of LOVE, of family, of things that happened in our family's lives. They were lessons that someday he might be able to learn from for his own life--called experience. These LOVE LETTERS ultimately turned into text messages that I today send to family members on a random basis to all that have phones--five of six grandchildren, their parents, and my wife. My prayer is that I can give my family the opportunity to think positively, LOVE their God, LOVE one another, give to others, have a happy life, an abundant life, serve those they come in contact with, and make this Earth a better place to live!

They are watching how I treat my wife, Petey. They are watching how I treat other family members. They are watching how I treat my co-workers. They are listening to the words that I speak, the way I respect others, the way I keep my mouth shut, and, from time to time, the way I put my foot in it.

They are watching my actions. The way I provide for my family. The way I provide for others. The way I perform "Random Acts of Kindness." The way I give God thanks for all our blessings. The way I praise them. The way I participate in their lives. The way I call them, just to see how they are doing. The way I hug them. The way I tell them, "GOD LOVES YOU." The way I tell them, "I LOVE YOU!"

They are watching and they are learning!

They are also watching as I mess up and make mistakes. Then, during those times, they are attentive to the way I say, "I'm sorry. Please forgive me." And how I make it right, to the best of my ability.

They are also watching when someone else messes up or makes mistakes. Do they blame others? Do they make excuses? Do they run from the issue? They are watching--all are watching!

How are you setting a positive example for your family? What will you start doing differently to improve your family tree? When will you change your family tree for the better . . . forever? How will the next three generations remember you?

YOU make a difference in others' lives!

CHAPTER 4:
LOVE is the most positive emotion on earth . . . and LOVE is within YOU!

When my siblings and I were seniors in high school, my parents had a formal dinner on our birthday. It was the only time that I recall my mother taking out the crystal, china, and silver from the dining room cabinet. A white linen tablecloth, white linen napkins, and candles topped off the amazing dinner that she meticulously created for the family.

It was during this dinner feast that my mother, father, and siblings celebrated our birthday during the senior year of high school. We also received our "Family Ring."

My grandfather passed away when my father was sixteen years young. Dad received his ring at his death and wore it until the day he died at eighty-six years young. When I was a child, I would play at my dad's office. In the back right corner of the middle drawer of his desk was a small manila envelope. It had two replicas of the Fite Family Ring. Little did I know that my parents would ultimately be giving them to my brother Carl and me. Nor did I know that my father would ultimately design a diamond ring for his two daughters.

The Fite Family Ring is made of the precious metal of gold. It is round signifying the family circle with three red rubies representing the blood of Christ. The three stones signified the

LOVE Chapter from the Bible, 1 Corinthians 13. Faith, Hope, and LOVE--the larger center stone in the middle of the ring signified *"the greatest of these is LOVE."*

Dad had incredibly beautiful penmanship and wrote us a personal letter about life and LOVE. The letter is a keepsake that I still have and read from time to time. Why? To keep me grounded, to remind me where I came from, and to take seriously my responsibility to others. Faith, Hope, and LOVE--the greatest of these is LOVE!

The family ring has now been given to my father's children, grand-children and great-grand-children. Dozens of these rings have been distributed on their high school senior year birthday. The tradition lives on.

Have you known of a family where the mother and/or father never tell their children, "I LOVE YOU"? A family where perhaps they were never told these caring words by their parents so they, in turn, didn't tell their children?

What is your legacy? What is your family legacy going to leave behind? Who is going to change NOW?

There is no better "receiving" feeling than when your spouse, children, or grandchildren send you a text and write, "I LOVE YOU!" There is no better "giving" feeling than when you send your spouse, children, or grandchildren a text and write, "I LOVE YOU!"

Hugs are a form of LOVE! Hugs with a whisper, "I LOVE YOU!" are even a greater feeling--the most amazing feeling from one person to another. My father used to teach us that you need twelve hugs a day, just to keep up! Some of us are undernourished when it comes to hugs!

Petey and I have a 27-foot gallery/hallway leading from our condo front door. Every morning, she walks me to the door, we hug, and we both say, "I LOVE YOU!"

How do you treat those you LOVE? How do you show your LOVE? Do you say, "I LOVE YOU" to those you LOVE? How often?

Zig Ziglar said that motivation is like bathing, you need it every day! LOVE is like bathing, you need it, and you need to give LOVE every day!

LOVE--without any doubt--is the GREATEST EMOTION ON THIS EARTH!

Call, text, or email someone you LOVE right now, or at least today. Tell them, "I LOVE YOU!"

YOU make a difference in others' lives!

CHAPTER 5
YOU are made to work . . .
to contribute to others and to the world!

Work ethic is like a muscle. Everyone has the ability, yet each person must engage and exercise it to be useful and reach their full potential.

The secret to having a strong work ethic is "habit!" It is getting up in the morning, even when you don't want to or need to. It is going to work. It is doing the things one must do to be successful. It is contributing to others through your work.

In my fifty-plus years in real estate including brokerage, mortgage, insurance, title, property management, and relocation, I have seen thousands of REALTORS come and go. For thirteen years I had the privilege of teaching real estate in private schools, colleges, universities, conventions, and conferences, as either an instructor or guest speaker. For most of my career, I volunteered in the local, state, and national association of REALTORS. I have also volunteered and served on the board of directors of various organizations and non-profits.

Bottom line, I have seen people who are passionate about their careers and have incredible work ethics. I have also seen those who are lazy, have poor character, lack interest, and have low to no participation.

What category do YOU fall in? Whom will you be from this day forward?

The failure rate in real estate brokerage is over 70% within the first twelve to twenty-four months and over 80% in five years. This is an alarming rate! An individual in Texas at this time must take 180 hours of classroom instruction, then pass the state exam. This can take weeks or months and it is approximately a $2,000 cash investment. Yet, most don't make it in their new career once they start!

Why? I have narrowed it down to three *Secrets to Success* or failure.

1. **SHOW UP** – REALTORS are independent contractors for the most part, not W-2 employees. About one-third of them are getting into the profession for "flexibility." Yet, the vast majority simply do not "show up!" For the first time in their working lives, no one is going to call them at 9:05 am (when they should be at work at 9:00 am) and say, "Are you OK? Is there a reason you aren't at work? Is there a reason you didn't call in?" REALTORS are business owners who can set their own schedules. Let me be clear, flexibility does NOT mean you don't have to go to work! If they amble into the office about 10:00 am, leave for lunch at 11:30. and go home at 3:00 pm, the actual work time is three to six hours at the most. Therefore, they fail!

   The world in which we live today has become a place that does not encourage work. As a matter of fact, it discourages work! Look at the number of holidays, vacation days, and personal time off (PTO) days, which are given in today's workplace, especially in the federal government. It is amazing that anything gets accomplished. Work gets completed by those who dedicate themselves to getting up every day and going to work!

Do you go to work on time? Do you show up?

2. **WORK WHEN YOU SHOW UP** – Many choose a company that has the illusion of an extremely high percentage of commissions (REALTORS are primarily commission-only sales professionals--100% of nothing is still nothing). The Texas Real Estate Commission required courses DO NOT teach an individual how to succeed in the real estate business. The courses DO teach an individual these four things:
    a. How to stay out of the courtroom--protect the public. (Which is important)
    b. How to stay out of jail--protect the public and don't commit fraud. (Which is important)
    c. Definitions--What is a note, deed of trust, deed, metes, and bounds, etc., the talk of real estate. (Most of which will never be used in their real estate career)

d. How to pass at least some of the state exam. (A must to practice real estate)

What the commission doesn't teach a new agent includes, but is not limited to:

a. What to do to build a career
b. How to build a business
c. How to manage a commission-only budget
d. What capital (money) is needed to succeed
e. How to save and pay income taxes
f. What training is needed to succeed
g. What support is needed to succeed
h. What people around you are needed to succeed (positive team culture)
i. What leadership is needed to succeed
j. What tools are needed to succeed
k. What marketing is needed to succeed
l. What "experience" is needed to succeed

The items listed above are critical to the success of a REALTOR, but there is so much more to learn--a lot more! I believe all these things are needed to be successful in any career. Just imagine if you work for someone else and they provided you with the information above. Imagine how your life, career, and family would improve if you worked toward the "big picture" of your career instead of just "showing up."

A person with a license to practice real estate shows up, they don't know what to do next, so they don't do anything--then they quit showing up. And the failure cycle continues.

3. **YOU ARE WHAT YOU THINK ABOUT** - Fill your mind with positive thoughts, and successful ideas! Pay attention to what you watch on television and hear on the radio. Listen to positive podcasts, uplifting music, and inspirational audiobooks. When you fill your mind with bad stuff, your body puts out the bad stuff. As Henry Ford said, "If you think you can, or if you think you can't, you're right!"

Your positive mental attitude is critical to your own success!

Some food for thought:
What do you like to do? What is your passion? What are your God-given gifts? What are you good at doing? Are you happy with your job? Do you have either a job or a career? What is your "WHY?" What is your passion?

God has given you a talent. Remember, He has a master plan for your life. He also gave you "free choice." This free choice may be why you are in the "job" that you are in. Is it merely a place to make a living (which is very important) for you and your family? YOU have been given GIFTS. Are you utilizing your gifts?

Question – If money did not matter, what would you do? (Yes, I realize money does matter) Do you like working with your hands? Building things? Fixing stuff? Do you like to draw or paint? Helping others? Would you work with or volunteer with a charity, non-profit or religious organization? Encouraging or coaching other people? Creating jobs for others? Inventing things? Helping others make decisions that are good for them to make like in sales? How can you help contribute to others?

There are books written on finding your niche or purpose. Find one, two, or three and read them. Think about what you like to do! Find your WHY!

Find your PASSION. What would you do for free that would fulfill your life? Having passion is when you wake up in the morning and look forward to your day. Passion is doing what you do when you LOVE what you do!

One of the messages my wife taught in her speaking career is, *"Work is only work when you would rather be doing something else."* I am not sure who taught her this or if it was her original thought. What matters is that it shows passion for a career, life's calling, God's calling.

What are you really good at doing? I mean really good! Each one of us, has gifts, both strengths, and weaknesses. Build on your strengths, and find others to do what you don't like to do as they need to follow their passion too! Build and refine your strengths and passion through education, attending classes and seminars, reading, listening to podcasts, and learning from others, and your own life experiences. Learn from every facet of life.

PASSION makes you get up in the morning. It's what gives you purpose in your life. What do you like to do? What are your interests? It encourages you to make the extra call if you are in sales, arrive at your career early, work later than required, and in return, you provide extra quality in your product or service to your clients, company, and career. Passion puts a smile on your face each day doing what you love in your job or career.

At age eleven I started my first career. Little did I know that it was the beginning of a career path. My father hired me to clean the office, just like he had done with my two sisters and brother. Dad had business cards printed with his company logo on them and my name. My title was, "Vice President in charge of Maintenance." In other words, I cleaned the office each week for $40 per month. My first paying job. On weekends during the growing season, I mowed yards for neighbors and my father's property listings.

Dad's secretary for over thirty years was my Aunt Eppie. Eppie was the second daughter of nine children and sister to my mother, Dene. When I cleaned the office, Eppie would go behind me and ask me, "See that, how can you clean it better? Did you clean ___? Did you do your best? YOU can do better! Now do it!" She and my father taught me to be the best I could be in all that I did! And I continue that work ethic to this very day. I pray by writing this book, I can inspire you as my Aunt Eppie inspired me to be the best that I can be each and every day!

Without me realizing it they were teaching the readers of this book WORK ETHICS! This includes me, you, my children, grandchildren, friends, and relatives. They also taught me that all jobs are important-- whether cleaning toilets, washing windows, mowing yards, helping people find a home for their family, creating jobs, or caring for and serving others to always be the best that they can be!

If your parents and mentors did not teach you strong work ethics, it is up to you to improve your family tree. When? NOW! The world needs YOU! The world needs you to be the best that you can be at whatever your chosen career might be!

YOU make a difference in others' lives!

CHAPTER 6
Be FREE from debt . . .
FREE your body, mind, and soul!

In high school, I took a class on personal finance. In my first semester of college, I received an "incomplete" in accounting. Not completing accounting back then taught me not to play cards in the student center and skip class. Let me say that through personal finance I have learned how to live my life by managing my money.

PERSONAL FINANCE – Every high school should teach this to all students! Before I married in June of 1972 at eighteen years young (too young in hindsight), I purchased a house by assuming a loan with $200 down and a $148 monthly payment.

I earned my real estate license that same year on March 1 and went into real estate sales full time. I had $600 in the bank that I had saved from my high school job shampooing and laying carpet after school and on weekends. By July 1, I was broke. Luckily my "then wife" (whom I am friends with today) took a summer job while she continued her college education and was able to pay our bills for the summer until my real estate career took off in September of 1972.

During the first five months of my career, I made a total of $152.50. Fortunately, I landed a doctor prospect who wanted to buy a home and sell one. He was only available at night, and we would drive the streets viewing homes until 2:00 am many evenings. After weeks of looking and submitting offers on many houses, even an attempt to trade one of his apartment houses for a home, he was able to purchase a house. I will always be indebted to him for teaching me another lesson on work ethic. **Do what you must (legally and ethically) to get the job done, no matter the hours that you spend--learn from every experience.** As it is said, "The rest is history." This sale and the listing and sale of his previous home launched my career in real estate.

At that time, I started an "emergency fund." I would never be broke again! My first year in real estate was from July -December and I earned $7,600. We saved $3,500 and put it in the bank.

THE EMERGENCY FUND - Because I worked in commission-only sales, it was imperative that I had cash to fall back on--so I would never be in that same no-money position again! I started this emergency fund with the $3,500. Then it grew to $5,000, then over time to $10,000. As I purchased rental properties, it grew to cover any unexpected property needs. When in a commission-only sales career, you should have at least six months of expenses saved up. Presently, my wife and I have twelve months because of the rental properties we own.

Later in life, we discovered Dave Ramsey. I highly recommend listening to his radio show or podcasts. Dave recommends an emergency fund of three to six months of your monthly expenses. We introduced him to our company in 2011 offering *Financial*

Peace University (FPU) tuition reimbursements to our agents or employees who would pay for the course, take it, and bring in the receipt and certificate of completion. That year over one hundred of our professionals took the course. We made a standing offer that anyone in our company could take the course. At this writing, we have six certified FPU instructors internally! Over the years, we have "changed the family tree security" of hundreds of families forever!

In March 2020, COVID changed our world. This pandemic hurt many people, including financially. Many had not been managing their money well and were left with a lot of debt and significant financial issues.

Our company immediately went into "recession mode."
As real estate is certainly a cyclical business, we didn't know what was going to happen. Luckily, by July 2020, the real estate market rebounded. By the end of the year, we were able to reward our valued employees and their families with a one-time bonus for sticking with our company and their hard work. In addition, we offered our real estate professionals, all employees of all the Judge Fite Companies, and their adult children, Ramsey+ courses for the year 2021. We purchased the entire program for everyone in advance. In 2021 we had 552 new users of Ramsey+ in our company. Lives and family trees were changed forever. When you listen to Dave Ramsey's radio, YouTube, or podcasts, you will hear people do a "Debt Free Scream!" And yes, we now have a "Debt Free Scream" offered to anyone in the company

during our monthly ZOOM company update meetings.

DEBT – Never be a "slave to the lender." When we borrow money, that is exactly what is happening! My recommendation is, to start listening to Dave Ramsey NOW! Buy his book *"The Total Money Makeover."* Subscribe to Ramsey+ for his courses and his app today. His programs will change your life and your family's legacy.

As Dave Ramsey says, *"Live today like no one else, so tomorrow you can live and give like no one else!"*

As for me, I have not had a car payment for over forty years. I have paid off my credit cards every month for over fifty years. I had a goal to be debt free of all mortgages by age sixty-six and achieved it by sixty-five and a half years of age. No consumer debt, no student loans for my kids' education--only mortgages. Once I heard about Dave Ramsey and we took Financial Peace University, my wife and I paid off our condo, our lake house, and our rental properties--all debt-free and now receiving "mailbox money." Mailbox money is where you receive income on a regular basis because you invested money throughout your life. Then, when you have the right investments, you receive money monthly or quarterly. This is money over and above what you earn in your job or career.

Being debt free has allowed us to "live and give" like no one else! We have boosted our giving. In 2017, our company founded the *Judge Fite Charitable Foundation* (JFCF). The purpose of JFCF is to help people in emergency need who are affiliated with any of our 1,000+ real estate professionals. The JFCF has helped people whose house burned, a loved one passed with no funds for the burial, a service dog for a child and so much more. Life happens to people and the JFCF is there to help them by delivering checks within 24-48 hours. The recipients of the grants can be clients, people they know, friends, family, or people they hear about in the community--they are the originators of the requests for grants from the foundation.

My wife and I have worked with the JFCF board of directors to set up an endowment account that we, and others, will fund over the next ten years. This account will be invested and 85% of the growth will be placed in the JFCF operating account for grants. The 15% growth will remain in the investment account to allow for fluctuations in the financial market and inflation.

Bottom line, being debt free has allowed us to "live and give" like no one else!

Just think what this world would be if everyone was debt free and all of us were givers, not takers!

YOU make a difference in others' lives!

CHAPTER 7
BEGIN . . . the rest is easy!

My friend Brian Buffini owner of the largest real estate training and coaching company in the world has a podcast, *"The Good Life Podcast."* Yes, Brian is Dermot's brother who challenged me to write this book. At the end of each interview with his guests, Brian asks several questions. One of the questions is, "What is the best advice you have ever been given?"

There is no question in my mind that the best advice I have ever been given is from my father, Judge B. Fite. He said, ***"BEGIN . . . the rest is easy!"***

Dad even had a brass sign on the wall in his office mounted on a wooden background that displayed this quote, *"BEGIN . . . the rest is easy!"*

Throughout my career, I have seen people prepare to prepare to prepare to start someday. These people are called "over-preparers." The world is full of us! This is why reading, listening to "positive stuff," coaching, and personal development is so important for a person's life. *BEGIN . . . the rest is easy!*

Some people say, "I must know everything before taking action." Well, I have news for you. You will never know everything about any subject. NEVER! The world, the country, your state, your locality, your profession, and your family will never stay constant. There will never be a perfect time. You simply must *BEGIN* . . . *the rest is easy!*

I have been in the real estate brokerage and services business for my entire adult life, and I am still learning something new all the time! The world is ever-changing. Your business is ever-changing. Your family is ever-changing. Your life is ever-changing. If you wait to know "everything" you will never act. *BEGIN* . . . *the rest is easy!*

Procrastination is a dirty word in my mind. When you put off until tomorrow what you can do today, this is procrastination. Most importantly, you just lost a day of your life! You just lost a sale! You just lost a relationship! You just lost a _____, fill in the blank. *BEGIN* . . . *the rest is easy!*

Have you ever had a project that you dreaded? Of course, we all have. You put off starting, then your mind started telling you how hard it would be. You started thinking there is no way to complete the project, thinking about all you needed to have before starting, and the help you needed from others. And then, finally, you started anyway! In hindsight, you discovered that it wasn't nearly as difficult as you thought. You did in fact complete the project! You didn't need all that stuff! YOU DID IT! *BEGIN* . . . *the rest is easy!*

How do we help our children and grandchildren, peers, and supervisors with projects? Do we allow them to default on a project or not complete what they started and committed to? What are we teaching them? Shouldn't we hold them accountable to BEGIN, to do their best, and to finish the project? How about those whom we work with in our business? How about those we coach? How about those we lead? BEGIN . . . the rest is easy!

YOU make a difference in others' lives!

CHAPTER 8
Worry . . . is wasted mind power!

My mother, Dene Fite, always said to us kids, "Worry is wasted mind power!" Thanks, Mom!

As the world turns, as our country, state, city, business, and family turns, and as we turn, "STUFF" happens! In the previous chapter, we talked about taking charge and starting our tasks. Now we are talking about "STUFF!"

The world is full of stuff going on. The media is certainly biased on their particular channel's beliefs; it is no longer true journalism. Social media has taken hold of the "stuff" and spins it out of control in the minds of people, adding to the negativity, the "worry" of people, and things they have no control over. The vast majority of the world's happenings are out of your and my individual control.

Every morning before I get out of bed, I acknowledge my daily affirmations. I say to my God three things: 1) I ask Him to help me achieve my personal mission statement; 2) I recite the serenity prayer; 3) I ask Him to help me live by our company's five core values.

The Serenity Prayer: *God, give me the serenity to accept the things I cannot change, the courage to change the things I can, and the wisdom to know the difference.*

So many people allow outside forces they have absolutely no control over to rule their life. They worry about things they have no power to influence or control. They focus on things that are "over or under their pay grade."

This worry sometimes turns into jealousy, gossip, and drama. All of which are very destructive to others, to an organization, to our world, and to the individual that executes any of these behaviors. We all do it to a certain extent. Why? We are all human.

What is important is that we get involved in issues we can influence. Whether it is donating to build water wells for those who don't have clean drinking water, volunteering at a homeless shelter, or cleaning up after a natural disaster. We can always give a helping hand to someone in need. There are certainly things that you and I can do, individually and together, to make this world a better place! What will you do to serve others?

This chapter is to help us keep in mind the things that we have no influence over as well as how we can make a difference and not sit idly by and worry. We can vote for our preferred candidate, but we cannot dictate the way they will lead our city, state, or country. We can watch the way they act and lead so we can vote differently or the same in the next election. We can write them letters or emails and let them know our beliefs to give them guidance. We can pray for them.

We cannot keep them from making "terrible" decisions. Nor can we worry that their decisions will guide our lives in a bad direction. We must take responsibility for our own actions, set our own goals, and act to have a responsible life that contributes to the good in the world and to others.

We cannot and should not worry to the point that it makes us stand still and freeze. Nor should these outside factors affect our attitude in a negative way. A negative attitude is a relationship buster, a family buster, and a friend buster. When we let outside forces rule our attitude, we open the door for bad things to happen in our lives.

We should not become a "victim" by blaming everything and everyone else for our problems. Victims have a way of not taking responsibility for their own actions. Being a victim can cost us our mental and physical health. This can cause relationships, friendships, and families to break apart.

It has been said, *"We spend a whole lifetime worrying about what other people think . . . until someday we realize how seldom they do."* This is an amazing quote. We worry about what others think. We lose sleep over it. We repeat it over and over and over in our minds. STOP! NOW! Stop worrying. While you are worrying about "stuff" and what others are thinking about you, life is passing you by! People are too busy thinking about themselves, not you. Why waste time on worry when you could use the same energy on positive thoughts?

In the Bible, Philippians 4:6 says: "Do not be anxious about anything, but in every situation, by prayer and petition, with thanksgiving, present your requests to God."

Don't worry about those things you cannot change or do not have influence over. If you are a Christian, give those worries to God. Then determine what you can change or influence and develop a plan and take action!

So, what is the solution? Take control of your own life! Share your positive experiences with those you can serve. Give your God-given gifts to others. Make a positive difference in your own life so you can make a positive difference in others' lives.

YOU make a difference in others' lives!

CHAPTER 9
Ask questions . . .
LISTEN to the answers!

The art of communication is asking questions and listening to the answers. It has been proven that when we talk with others when we are asking questions, we are actually thinking of the next question we will ask instead of listening to the answers others are giving.

Have you ever been with someone who talked about themselves during a brief conversation or maybe an entire evening and they never asked anything about you? They were so self-absorbed or probably so insecure, that they did not think of asking about your story. Your background, struggles, tenacity, will, beliefs, family, dreams, or ambitions did not even cross their mind.

A consultant our company had many years ago taught me one of the best questions I have ever thought to ask when interviewing someone. His question was, *"Go back to high school and bring me up to date. What have you been doing?"* Then LISTEN to the answer! You will learn more in two-to-three minutes about an individual than you could from a general conversation.

Since learning this question, my wife and I have taken it to a whole different level. When you go out to dinner with strangers, ask the question. When you meet a prospective client, ask the question. When you meet your daughter's date, ask the question. And then, of course, LISTEN to the answer! You will learn a lot! Everyone has a story.

Listen to others. You can learn from anyone, everyone you meet. Sometimes, you will learn what to do. Sometimes, you will learn what not to do. My father said to me, "Listen to smart people." Good advice!

Most "smart" people are experienced people. People who have succeeded in life, family, and the pursuit of happiness. They are also people who have failed. Zig Ziglar said, *"Failure is an event, not a person."* Failures are a step to success when you take time to learn from them. You should learn from every experience--when you succeed and when you don't.

Listen to others. They have been where you are. They have been where you have been. They will go where you will go. Seek them out. Some call these people trusted advisors or mentors. Maybe your mentors are with you for a lifetime. They may meet you for coffee or give you guidance over coffee or a meal. Learning from someone who has walked the path that you wish to take will save you energy, time, and a lot of money throughout your life.

Listen when learning. Most educators are called to their profession. Sometimes we remember the teachers we had in elementary, middle, high school, and college. We think about something they taught us or the positive impact they had on our life.

I confess I wish I had paid more attention in school, listened to my teachers more, learned from my homework assignments, studied for tests that were given, and most importantly, I wish I had implemented all that I did learn!

Dad gave me another piece of advice, *"Before you go to lunch with someone, ask to see their 1099 (W-2)."* He was attempting to teach me that if you go to lunch with others, be careful about the advice they are giving you. In other words, be careful whom you listen to. People will tell you how you can or how you can't accomplish your goals. They will tell you what is wrong vs. what is right about life, your decisions, your career, your boss, your wife or husband, etc.

Whom do you listen to? Who gives you advice? Who cares about you? Who helps you grow? Just as it is your choice of being happy every day, you have the option of learning from every experience, every conversation, and every person. Yet you must determine what is good to learn from to make a positive difference versus learning from negative, unsuccessful people. Whose choice is it? YOURS!

Listen, learn, give, and LOVE so you can make a difference in others' lives.

YOU make a difference in others' lives!

CHAPTER 10
Over communicating is KEY . . .
Don't under-communicate and regret it!

Creating a culture in a company is easy when you are small. As you grow, it becomes more difficult to maintain, communicate, and live the culture you and your people have developed.

What is a "company" culture? What is a "corporate" culture? What is a "sales" culture? What is a "family" culture? What is a "caring" culture? What is a "cut-throat" culture? What is a "non-culture?"

Communication is the foundation of culture. It is cascading messaging from the leaders of the company. For a family, it is communication from the matriarch and patriarch of the family.

In our business, we have sales professionals, staff, leaders, and managers that motivate and operate our various offices, departments, and companies that we own. The #1 complaint from clients throughout my fifty-plus-year career, without a doubt, is, "I haven't heard from my agent/salesperson/contractor, etc." Communication is paramount to excellent customer service.

We teach our agents to set up a defined day of the week, either morning or afternoon to give a weekly update on the status of a listing or sale. Then we go on to say, "If the client calls you every six days, you call them every five days. If the client calls you every four days, you call them every three days. If the client calls you every 3 hours, you call them every two hours." If the client thinks they must initiate the call to their agent, they do NOT think you are communicating with them. YOU must initiate the call and communicate—always!

As for me, our company has grown from one office with eight people to well over 1,000 people. Communication in a smaller group is certainly easier. Communication in this large group is very difficult at best. It takes a conscious effort.

So, how do we communicate in today's society? Email, postal mail (including personal notes, letters, and postcards), texts, phone calls, in-person, meetings, seminars, training, rallies, and recognition/awards events.
USE ALL OF THE ABOVE and more!

When appropriate, we should always ask the client, "In what media do you like to be communicated?" Then deliver on that method plus at least one other type! If they want text, communicate via text, and then call them from time to time. If they prefer email, call or text them every now and then. However, if they don't want to be communicated with in a certain way, be sure to respect and uphold their wishes.

Under promise and over deliver on communication!

Over the years we have been criticized by REALTORS saying, "I didn't know that! Why didn't you tell me? I never received that email, text, call, letter, etc."

Come to find out they didn't fully pay attention to the various ways we communicate with over 1,000 people in more than twenty different locations. They missed meetings where communication takes place, didn't listen or read the PowerPoint slides when they attended the meetings, and didn't read communications that were sent out via email, text, or social media groups.

We have been criticized for giving too much information too fast, especially by new agents and employees. As a company, we do take this all in, listening to suggestions, reading survey results, and ideas, then we adapt whenever possible.

Below are a few ways we communicate and reach out to our agents and employees to make sure information is conveyed and received:
1. Not everyone reads what they are emailed the first or even the second time, therefore, most communication must be sent at least three times to reach the audience.
2. Some do not read; therefore, we verbally communicate via regular meetings presented throughout the company.
3. When appropriate in small, short communications, texting works.
4. When a select few are involved, a personal phone call is made. This is the only format that we are certain is received as we talk directly to the individuals or leave a voice mail--

and, of course, we are hoping they listened to their voice messages.

As for too much information in a short period of time which several new REALTORS have mentioned, an alternative is to spread it out over a longer period of time.

The issue is that many want information today, while others may not need it for a week, a month, or a year. There is no way in our business, or in most businesses, to know when one will "need" the info.

Think of the solution like a book. We read the book, we don't memorize the book, yet, when needed, we can revisit the book and look up the answer.

I have found throughout my career, with my family, and in life, too much information quickly far outweighs giving less information over a longer period of time. Of course, the best solution is to give more information than less--over-communicating versus under-communicating.

YOU make a difference in others' lives!

CHAPTER 11
YOU have a choice every day . . .
be HAPPY, have a GREAT DAY!

What kind of day are you having today? A good day? A bad day? A fair day?

Every day we have an individual choice in our life--our attitude and mood. There are "things" in life, in business, in families that try to disrupt our day--make it worse, mess it up. Yet, how we approach these "trials" and how we allow them to affect our attitude is 100% up to us.

Ever had a bad day? Of course, we all have good and bad days. How did you handle the bad day? Did you let it bother you from the inside? Did you let it affect your personal relationships with others, even though they had nothing to do with the bad event that started the mood? Did you overreact with those who brought on the bad day? Did you take your internal problems out on others? How did you overcome the bad day or the bad situation?

How did you handle the good day? I would bet that it felt good emotionally, therefore, your attitude was good and the way you treated others was good too.

On this good day, did you allow small bad things to bother you? Or did you overlook those things that you could not affect anyway?

You and I have a choice every day! We can choose to make it a good day, regardless of how our parents, spouse, significant other, children, co-workers, boss, or clients treat us. No matter how they talk to us. No matter what they do to try and hurt us emotionally.

Sometimes, people let us down. How do you treat those that do not live up to your (or even their) standards? Do you keep it inside? Do you yell at them? Do you throw things? Do you abuse them emotionally or even physically? Do you run away and hide? Hopefully not.

I suggest that when people do let you down, you develop a plan of action. First, don't take the issue out on others. Second, develop a plan of communication. Third, have a private conversation with the individual. During this private conversation: Let them know that they mean a great deal to you. Then tell them, from your perspective, what happened, and how you feel they let you down. Next, communicate a possible solution, direction, or way to fix the issue. And then, agree to a plan of action moving forward. After each of these steps listen to the responses. LISTENING is the key to great communication. Ultimately, arrive at an agreement with solutions that allow you both to move forward or even agree to disagree.

Sometimes, WE let people down. We are not perfect. We are human. Yes, you and I can be the individual that lets others down. We do not treat others with respect, sometimes we discipline in public rather than in private. How do you recover from letting others down or making a mistake? First, learn from your mistake and do your best to not do it again. Second, admit that you messed up. Third, let others know what you learned from the mistake. Fourth, ask for their forgiveness.

YOU have a choice every day! It is your choice, no one else's. You own it! What kind of day do you choose to have today and every day? Are you going to have a great day, a good day, a fair day, or a bad day? I choose to have a GREAT DAY! How about YOU?

YOU make a difference in others' lives!

CHAPTER 12
ONE hour a day . . . read, study, and think!

Yes, it was at a Mexican restaurant in Dallas that my life would change forever. That is when my mother and father challenged me to "read, study, and think" an hour a day, five days per week, for the rest of my life.

I believe that this advice and challenge changed my life and the lives of others for the better--forever.

As I look back on my life, now for over fifty years I have been following their advice. I am a morning person. I like to wake up and "read, study, and think" early when my mind is fresh without interruptions. My phone is not ringing. Text messages and emails are not distracting me, and the opportunities and challenges of the day have not yet begun. It gives me a chance to reflect on what happened in the past and what or who I need to serve in the future. It is a time when I work "on my business," rather than in my business.

There are some days or even weeks that things get in the way of my hour per day. Yet, there are days when I will "read, study, and think" anywhere from two to five hours in a day. On average, I believe I put in over and above the five hours per week to self-improvement and developing the lives of family members, our companies, our community, and, hopefully, our world by reading, studying, and thinking for at least an hour per day.

I am not a strong reader. However, this is no excuse to not read. Charlie "Tremendous" Jones said, *"You will be the same person in five years as you are today except for the people you meet and the books you read."* So true!

At an early age, I was diagnosed with mixed dominance and dyslexia. Long before public education diagnosed learning differences in children, my mother realized that I had trouble learning to read. My parents spent thousands of hours and no telling how much money having me tested by professionals in child development. I attended special education classes every day after public school. I also took speed reading courses on Saturdays while my friends were playing sports and having fun. I often wonder where I would be if my parents had not invested time and money in me and my learning.

Mixed dominant is a condition where I am right-handed and right-footed but left-eyed and left-eared. In other words, the left side of my brain is in control of my hands and feet, and the right side of my brain is in control of my eyes and ears. Imagine how these crossed signals disrupt a person from learning. A mixed dominant person hears the teacher, sees the words, and writes what they learn yet it gets mixed up in their brain.

As a result, I read one word at a time, not phrases or sentences like most people. Therefore, I read very slowly.

There is always a saving grace for all disabilities. From every weakness comes strength. In my case, I have a very high retention rate of what I read. Additionally, I have an amazing capacity of implementing what I learn.

To quote my friend Brian Buffini once again, *"Education without implementation is merely entertainment."* I have been blessed with the ability to implement what I "read, study, and think" about in my spiritual, business, family, and personal life.

Dyslexia is mixing up letters and numbers in the wrong order. This includes reading backwards, (right to left v. left to right), skipping to new lines of copy midsentence while reading, typing, or writing backward, and more. Just in writing this book, I have to carefully type, read, then re-read to make sure words or letters are not backward or missing. Spell check is a great benefit!

The good news for anyone with a learning difference diagnosis, young or old, there are educational steps and programs as well as qualified professionals that can help them learn regardless of the disability. Listen to the professionals and take their advice. Who knows what contribution to the world someone with a learning difference will make!

I always have a book with me. Even with my reading issues, I still read a few pages every day. I learn from others who have lived their lives differently than I. You can do the same. It is a matter of making up your mind that you are going to learn from smart people. Level up your reading and level up your learning. By doing so, you will grow your life and grow it more abundantly.

Thanks to mom and dad for investing in me! Being my advocate! Challenging me! Believing in me!

Certainly, some days I wake up and have early appointments, meet others for breakfast, or am on an early morning flight.

On those days when something interferes with "my time," I merely find another time later that day or make up the time on a different day. For me, an airplane ride can be the most creative time that I have. No phone ringing, no text messages, no email--just uninterrupted time in which to *"read, study, and think."*

Try *"read, study, and think"* for thirty days. Select a book, and read a few pages, or a chapter a week. Get a yellow pad and write down your thoughts as you read. Take it one step further and purchase a journal to write your life's story--one day at a time. This is also a great time to work on a project during your uninterrupted time. You will be amazed at what comes to mind. New ideas arise, people come to mind that you need to contact, and services that you can provide to others come to the forefront. This is also a great time to plan out your day, week, month, year--your life!

YOU make a difference in others' lives!

CHAPTER 13
Classroom and world knowledge . . . ALWAYS keep learning!

As I mentioned in the previous chapter, my friend Brian Buffini says, *"Education without implementation is purely entertainment."* I have put it in this book twice because I believe it is so true! In my own life, I have attended a multitude of classes every year throughout my life to constantly broaden my knowledge. This was my promise to my mother and father when I quit college. They said, *"You never stop learning."*

I have witnessed people attend classes yet do not "show up" and pay attention. We give our new agents company homework assignments to help them grow their business. In week five of training, I ask, "Have you completed your first day of homework?" Time and again, only one-third of the class has completed the homework while two-thirds have not. Remember, real estate agents are independent contractors, not employees so it is up to them as to how successful they will be.

You must implement what you learn. You must take action! I will say it again:
"Education (listening and taking notes) without implementation is purely entertainment" -- Brian Buffini

Early in my career, I attended a seminar and the next day I walked into my father's office and complained about it. I said, "The speaker was boring, the speaker was not dressed properly, the speaker didn't have any handouts, the speaker didn't do this or didn't do that!" My father leaned back in his chair and said, "Son, it doesn't matter if the speaker is boring or what they are wearing. Your goal in every seminar or class is to find one idea that you will implement to help you sell one more house this year and every year throughout your career." My dad was very wise. From that day forward, and continued today, I am looking for **ONE IDEA** that I can implement from listening to others that I encounter. Everyone can teach me if I will only listen to them. **Everyone can teach you if you will only listen and learn.** They can teach what to do or what not to do!

Learn from others' experiences. Education by "experience" of others is very inexpensive. Education from your own experience is EXTREMELY EXPENSIVE! Listen to others as they talk about what works and what doesn't. However, be careful in taking people at "face value." Check and recheck data to make sure the information is factual.

In real estate, there are a lot of "get rich quick" schemes. Late-night TV is full of "no money down" infomercials that are luring people to buy seminars at a ridiculous price! Our agents and companies are besieged with novices who create havoc in our business for a short period of time. Don't get sucked in by these "work less and get rich" schemes!

When I obtained my real estate license and started my real estate business my dad gave me a book about how to set goals. This process was:

1. Think them out
2. Categories in which to set goals
   a. Spiritual
   b. Family
   c. Educational
   d. Career
   e. Financial
   f. Personal
3. Write them down
4. Make them realistic, yet stretchable
5. State them positively

Who should be a goal setter? YOU! Any seminar that is worth its weight teaches goal setting. It has been said, *"If you don't know where you are going, how do you know when you get there?"* Setting goals is not an exact science, it is a process of having a vision of short and long-term goals in all the categories stated above.

In our company, we use the Entrepreneurial Operating System as taught in the book *Traction* by Gino Wickman. Our company has a ten-year "Big, Hairy, Audacious Goal." We set three-year, one-year, and quarterly rocks. A 'rock' is a goal that must be completed above all others. We also have a Level 10 meeting each week in every office and department to keep us on track to reach our goals.

As my life has matured, our entire family has an annual meeting to discuss our estate and money matters. (Another great suggestion by Dave Ramsey.) My wife and I plan our lives in the yearly categories above. We continue to learn about goal setting as we attend The Buffini Company's MasterMind Conference in San Diego each August. During this conference, Brian has everyone in attendance--about 5,000 people--write down their goals.

What conferences will you attend each year? Will you plan out next year's educational training during this year's fourth quarter? Set your goals for next year? Plan your calendar? Schedule your activities to reach your goals?

In the end, it is your God-given choice. Your ability to have free will. What will you do with your free will?

YOU make a difference in others' lives!

CHAPTER 14
Money comes and money goes. . . it is the **PEOPLE** you touch and your **REPUTATION** you leave behind

There are many truths stated about money. And there are equally as many false statements made about money.

Some would say that money is evil. Some would say that women and men should not attempt to build wealth. Some would say that people with money are all kinds of bad things!

Personally, I do NOT agree with any of those statements above. I have had money and I have not had money. I like having money a lot more than not having it.

Money by itself has no value. It is a piece of paper or a digital amount in a bank account. Without people wanting goods and services, money has no value.

I have adopted Dave Ramsey's philosophy. The money that I have earned, saved, and accumulated is God's money. It is up to me to be a good steward of God's money.

"Money comes and money goes.
In the end, it is the people you touch and
your reputation you leave behind!"
Jim Fite

Each of us has the God-given challenge and opportunity to provide for our family. Food, shelter, and quality of life. To give back to our God and fellow man/woman. To help those who are less fortunate. Money by itself is not evil. The worship of money, and if harm is done with and through money, then money can become evil.

As stated earlier, I started working when I was eleven years young. I began mowing yards in the summer. Then in junior high and high school, I shampooed, repaired, and laid carpet after school and on the weekends. I earned money, blew through money, and saved money.

It was during this time that I watched a program on the actor and rancher Gene Autrey. As I recall, it stated that he saved 50% of everything he earned throughout his life. So, I started on that quest. For some reason, Gene's story stuck with me and helped mold my financial life moving forward! I did not save 50% of my income forever. I transferred that knowledge of wealth and have become an earner, saver, investor, and giver throughout my life.

At first, our father's company, Judge Fite Company, was small in size and located in a blue-collar area of the Dallas/Fort Worth Metroplex. My sister and I purchased his business in 1977 and let's just say there was no money remaining in the bank for a recession. While owning this business, we saved cash for the many up and down cycles of real estate brokerage. To date, we have SUCCEEDED through five recessions.

Skipping forward many years, our company saved several months of cash to carry us through the next recession. It certainly arrived in DFW in the fall of 2006. To this day 2007 - 2010 is known as the "Great Recession."

During this time, our company's gross income dropped by 52% and our company dollar dropped by 43%. We reduced expenses, took no pay out of our brokerage company for five years, and asked our company employees to reduce their base salaries. Our leadership team did everything in its power to succeed through this dismal period.

As I am writing this paragraph, no one knew that during this timeframe our company depleted 100% of our savings and borrowed 100% of our line of credit at the bank for which we had pledged personal assets and liability. The company was down to making payroll for two weeks and after that, we were not sure what the future held. By the grace of God, a lot of hard work, money in the bank at the beginning of the recession, a reduction of expenses, cooperation of our landlords and vendors, dedication by our people, and a productive spring real estate market, our income turned in the right direction.

On December 31, 2012, our company paid back every leader who had taken a reduction in their personal pay--every dime they had sacrificed for our company. What company would ever do this for their employees? When you join the Judge Fite Companies, you join the Judge Fite Family! Our company's Core Value #1 – Honesty and integrity; to ALWAYS do the right thing!

It was during this "Great Recession" that I realized, *"Money Comes and Money Goes. It is the people you touch and your reputation you leave behind."*

During these years, my family relationships were amazing. The care, support, and concern that my friends had for me and my family were what got me through on an emotional level. They were there for me and my wife through the hard times, the difficulties of business, the economy, and money issues. I can never repay them or express to them what their support meant to me personally and professionally. They believed in me! I believed in our people!

In this world there are givers and there are takers. I would like to think that during my adult life, I have been a giver. In the Bible, Acts 20:35 reads, *"It is better to give than receive."* I truly believe this to be true. Zig Ziglar said, "The more you give, the more you receive."

As for the people you touch, you and I meet many people every day. When we do, how do we treat them? Everyone deserves for us to treat them with respect.

How do we touch other people? A friendly smile, a helping hand, a listening ear--they all go a long way. In our company, we have an opportunity to help people buy homes, the place where they will raise their families, build wealth, entertain friends, and make memories. A home is an opportunity for our company to "touch lives" in a very special way. Through our company's process, we cover all aspects of purchasing a home or investment property. We "touch lives" in all our endeavors.

My wife and I tithe money to worthwhile religious, civic, and charitable organizations. Together, we also volunteer in many activities in the communities we serve.

In 1984, we founded a "teddy bear ministry" that has grown from collecting and distributing ten to now over 3,000 teddy bears to hospitals on Christmas Day each year. Even through the recent pandemic, we were able to quarantine the bears before delivering them to local hospitals for nurses and doctors to distribute. With every bear given to every patient, Santa, Mrs. Claus, and their elves say, "Merry Christmas, and God Bless you."

How will you touch people in a positive way today, tomorrow, and forever? What is your personal reputation with your world, your community, your friends, and your family? What have you done in your life that will be remembered by others? Have you made a "mark" on this world in a positive way?

Our reputation can be good, or it can be bad. What is yours? What have you done for others that made a positive impact on their life? Will people believe you were honest? Will you be known for having integrity? Did you do the "right thing" in all your actions?

YOU make a difference in others' lives!

CHAPTER 15
STRATEGIC planning and
DAILY Affirmations

At one point in my life, I was introduced to several regiments that would have a positive impact on me forever. Two of the most pivotal ones are strategic planning and daily affirmations.

In the early 1980s, the business initiative "Strategic Planning" was the buzz in business schools and associations throughout the United States. I was fortunate to hold a leadership chair in the Greater Dallas Association of REALTORS (now known as the MetroTex Association of REALTORS). During that period, I learned about strategic planning which changed the course of my business and life forever!

Sometime later, I attended a self-improvement seminar when the speaker asked, "Do you have a personal strategic plan?"

It was at that moment I began writing my personal and business strategic plan that included my Personal Mission Statement. It took several tweaks before I perfected my mission in life--for me. A few years later, I added to parts of it, and it has been in effect ever since.

At another seminar, I learned about daily affirmations. As I began to think about what

I needed to say to myself each morning, I put together the following plan:

<u>Every morning</u> before I get out of bed, I recite my daily affirmations. <u>Each night</u> I repeat these affirmations to help me relax as I fall asleep. Or, if I can't sleep in the middle of the night, I use them to help me fall back asleep.

Daily affirmations have become an important part of my life as to my relationship with my God, my attitude, my acceptance of people, my outlook on issues that arise, and so much more. They give me clarity about God, family, business, friendships, and people I meet on a regular basis. My affirmations are an important part of my well-being!

What I say to my God and myself daily:

God...

>   *Forgive me of my sins.*

>   *Forgive those who sin against me.*

>   *Help me achieve my personal mission each day--to be a positive example to others by spiritually living life, family values, giving to others, career success, and financial stability.*

I recite the Serenity Prayer:
>   *God, give me the serenity to accept the things I cannot change, the courage to change the things I can, and the wisdom to know the difference.*

Help me to live by my company's Core Values today and every day:
> **Core Value #1:** Honesty and Integrity--to ALWAYS do the RIGHT THING!
> **Core Value #2:** Dedication to our clients, profession, and community.
> **Core Value #3:** World Class Service.
> **Core Value #4:** Commitment to be goal focused and results driven.
> **Core Value #5:** Disciplined to do my job at its best.

These affirmations have shaped my life and kept me focused on what is important for my spiritual growth, staying grounded when family issues arise, caring for my fellow man/woman, growing my company in the right direction for our community, and prioritizing things that come up during any given day. They help me stay Christ-focused on and in everything that I do each and every day.

Thank you, God!

"YOU make a difference in others' lives!"

Made in the USA
Columbia, SC
20 March 2025